Radiant

For Connie —

you are Salt of the Earth and a Shining Light!

It's been so great seeing you again in Banff

love Katie

Copyright © 2019 Kate Marshall Flaherty

Except for the use of short passages for review purposes, no part of this book may be reproduced, in part or in whole, or transmitted in any form or by any means, electronically or mechanically, including photocopying, recording, or any information or storage retrieval system, without prior permission in writing from the publisher.

Canada Council for the Arts / Conseil des Arts du Canada

ONTARIO ARTS COUNCIL
CONSEIL DES ARTS DE L'ONTARIO
an Ontario government agency
un organisme du gouvernement de l'Ontario

Canadä

The publisher gratefully acknowledges the support of the Canada Council for the Arts and the Ontario Arts Council. The publisher is also grateful for the financial assistance received from the Government of Canada.

Front cover artwork: Bernadette Peets, "Luna," 2018, watercolour on paper, 4 x 6 inches. Artist website: www.bernadettepeets.com.

Cover design: Val Fullard

Library and Archives Canada Cataloguing in Publication

Title: Radiant : poems / Kate Marshall Flaherty.
Names: Flaherty, Kate Marshall, 1962– author.
Series: Inanna poetry & fiction series.
Description: Series statement: Inanna poetry & fiction series
Identifiers: Canadiana (print) 20190094346 | Canadiana (ebook) 20190094370 | ISBN 9781771336451 (softcover) | ISBN 9781771336468 (epub) | ISBN 9781771336475 (Kindle) | ISBN 9781771336482 (pdf)
Classification: LCC PS8611.L25 R33 2019 | DDC C811/.6—dc23

Printed and bound in Canada

Inanna Publications and Education Inc.
210 Founders College, York University
4700 Keele Street, Toronto, Ontario M3J 1P3 Canada
Telephone: (416) 736-5356   Fax (416) 736-5765
Email: inanna.publications@inanna.ca   Website: www.inanna.ca

MIX
Paper from responsible sources
FSC® C004071

Radiant

poems by
KATE MARSHALL FLAHERTY

inanna poetry & fiction series

INANNA Publications and Education Inc.
Toronto, Canada

*In memory of Deda, Gramma Lucy, Aunt Buffy, Bev, Margaret,
John, cousin Ann, Raymond, Rick and Jim, and for fellow sojourners
Catherine, Lois, Aunt Jane, cousin Maggie, Mary, Tanya, Jane,
Gerry, Priscila, all my friends at Wellspring.
And all our loved ones who have walked this cancer journey with us.*

*And for my dear friends and family,
who have all been shining lights along my journey,
whose names are written on my heart; you know who you are.
My gratitude is infinite as the stars.*

*There is a crack, a crack in everything
That's how the light gets in.*
　　　　　—Leonard Cohen, "Anthem"

Contents

MOTH PROJECT

Welcoming Angels	3
woman in winter	4
Skipped	6
Matrushka	7
Tumour	8
Mushroom	9
crimson	11
Dissolving *post surgery*	13
Salt-cured *wondering about chemo as a farm girl*	15
Chemo	16
Moth Project	18

SPACE AND LIGHT

With musical accompaniment	23
Fear, death, the whole shebang	24
Most things will never happen …	25
Lilac	26
Hairless	28
He Wishes for Snow	29
Light Up the Night	31
Moon Tides	33

Burn	36
Space and Light	38

SOPHIA

Triptych for my Children during Chemo	43
Frequently Asked Questions #3	45
Vox	48
Pelican	49
Ritual Blessing for my Womb	50
The magic is in the salt, they say	51
Photo: Old Woman Staring at Hands	53
winter moon at night	55
Sophia	56
Ode to my Vagina	59
Sprout *post chemo*	60

RADIANT

Medal of Honour	63
Book of Hours	65
From above	68
Poem to my Son on the Occasion of Dropping Out	70
…and this is the end of it…	72
Half Life	74
Son as Tree	75
Water Music	76

Moirai	77
Just a Titch	79
Ode to the Radium Girls	81
I will write me a love poem	83
Note to Self	84
You Can Lie Down Now	86
Radiant	87
Second Chance	88
Acknowledgements	91

Moth Project

*Between the last war
and the next one,
waiting for the northbound train
that travels by the river,
I sit alone in the middle of the night
and welcome angels.*

*…Welcome what is not my own;
glory on the top rung, coming down.*
—Pat Schneider, "Welcoming Angels"

Welcoming Angels

(with thanks to Pat Schneider)

I will not see cancer as an enemy
nor foreign intruder,
but a passenger pigeon, (not extinct),
flown from a roof box.

I thought I heard a flutter outside the glass,
guessed it was an angel,
(with wings and a horn),
wakening us to joy!

There was no rank
nor pecking order,
(no band 'round his ankle).
He wasn't lowly, was not proud

but clawed a scrap of paper
(by now I knew this was a dream, and
dreamed I woke before I read the note).

I knew what it said
without seeing the words,
the angel knew, as the bird,
a question:

will you wrestle with welcome,
learn homing?

woman in winter

i

i am on winter's
cold metal gurney

needles in my breast

biopsy bullet
gun to my chest

ii

i am winter
ice-grey
in solid mounds

dark boughs hang low

prey-birds crack
frozen seeds black
on white hospital blanket

iii

i am in winter-waiting

wanting to peer
past the sterile curtain

wishing results
will burst like maple buds—

neon against melting crust

warm earth, mud-rich
pregnant with seeds

crocus tips smiling
through sun-softened soil

iv

I am waiting on sudden
pastels from dull ground

lime-spritz freshness in the air
swirls in my chest
        I breathe in Easter light

Skipped

Sorry I missed
my *mammo*
a word on the calendar
skipped, passed over

I apologize, didn't go
pencil marks rubbed out
covered by lists

Forgive my not recalling—
reminders pinned to corkboard
with a red star

Regret now a year has passed
cycles missed
chance gone

I turn to chalk, can't
forgive myself
for this
wish to wipe the slate—

Matrushka

This has been harder on my mom,
and no wonder, the wrong order of it.

Listening to her long distance,
I comforted her comforting,
cried when I hung up.

I took up a novena
to love's mother—
imagine her buried child.

A Russian doll, innermost—
a mother outside me, one within—

a nesting

going back to a child again,
trusting that inner mother

to grow old
be still and know.

Tumour

Nestled in dense flesh
I, ominous orb
pearled myself larger
in soft oyster folds

I stayed silent
under the sea

Were you listening
to what bubbled up?

I was unknown
all those seasons of waves,
starting as a grain of sand—
no more grit than salt—

Swelling, I had no scent
of green before rain,
no shape or weight, just
mass of cells feeding like fish

By the time you saw me--
bright as a silver lure in an ocean mound,
I shone out from darkness

I chose to grow
in your bosom, for with it
you nourished children
and the world—

Mushroom

A dream: breathtaking
this mushroom garden
sprouting from each arm.

Tender white enoki shoots
with tree frog finger pads
at the top, cream buttons
with brown under-umbrellas.

Am I dreaming I'm awake
like Alice meeting the caterpillar,
hookah on his toadstool?

A smooth stone base
for each burst of fungi—
polished and flat,
spore or root? Or
a small rock on which
nature built her mushroom church.

How did this night soil
garden grow in me?

Recalling the puzzling labyrinth—
the way in is the way out—

spiraling keyhole
spread before the cathedral—

a place to meditate
at centre, leave the marketplace behind.

Mushrooms grow in darkness and shit,
yet their magic is medicine.
Cancer's a mushroom—
fearsome, fantastic.

I grasp the ebony stone, pull—
the long tendrils of fungus
slide lovely in one piece
clean out of my arm,
one, the other—

a bouquet in the sun.

crimson

red dust mountain on Mars—
ruffled collar of craters
crusted with dried magma
scabbing to points
curled and rusted metal

mount Vesuvius through a looking glass—
telescopes towards Emerge

into tiny tremblings
imperceptible as threads
in a petri dish

chill air stilling
kaleidoscope of metal gurneys
greens, sneakers, beeping gadgets

everything microscoping
into this one gaping puncture
angry blood
congealing into a rage
of sore flesh

erect in shock
a hunch of open skin
screams for sutures

black stitch-thread

sterile scissors lifeless
on a tray

latex gloves
snap a blue NASA frequency
on a distant monitor
black and white bug-static alien
in this volcanic vortex

flesh erupting
sucking me into
its fiery core

Dissolving
post surgery

You are sipping
a hot mug coddled
in hungry hands—
cocoa, honey,
goat milk steamed

on this quilted bed
a woollen sweater, books,
prayer cards, beads,
a plate of dates

under bitter chocolate froth
the scent of lilies
cream roses in a bowl
of clear water by the bed

a glint of sun in the glass
base trembling in baby's breath

you breathe in
the saint-scents in their vase,
warm milk, dried blood
holding tight the queries—
chlorine pool, teen smokes,
rage, resentment, mold—

Exhale, release

bits of dark camino
float to the edges,
cling to the cup.

Salt-cured
wondering about chemo as a farm girl

this taste is not just salt-and-soda,
but metallic
in its alien underscore.

I wish for sea brine, ocean froth,
sprinkles of Celtic
runes or Himalayan rock—

but this is not an earth-flavour.

I pour a palm-ful of seasonings into bone broth,
crush the herbs, wince
the garlic in a shiny press, stir—
nourishment rises in soup-steam.

I smell a bile rising
from somewhere sterile –
white, acrid—a steely
contrast to dirt-and-sand crumbles
moist and fecund
unbleached
beige and salmon.

Two medicines mingle.

Chemo

Phony conviction. Sterile.
I need to believe
in this red-electric juice
stung into my veins,
persuade my imagination
it's elixir. My faith
in healing is real—
I've seen convincing
proofs, known mysteries of light.

I've witnessed convicts
set free, jail bars
flung open; a brightness
quickening in each cell.

I've seen the earthy shroud
left in a mound

held a burst-open chrysalis
in my palm

have prayed
and been still,
sat like a hermit
in my space,
quiet, reverent—
even my fear
convinced me of one thing: love.

And so I will see you
ruby drug
as liquid love—

trust you are spreading
the good news.

Moth Project

Here at Bungle-Owen—
Christmas Eve dinner with cousins
at table in the cabin.

I wait all evening 'til seated,
stare at the cut-glass ornament
       in the bottom of my cup.

I notice my brother's first—
a cream-swirled goose,
       slender neck and red-dot eye.

This year mine is a moth,
stained-glass wings
forest colours,
thick ribbed body
       two tiny feelers at the head.

This is magic.
I am inside the cup
amid twinkling string of lights,
snow-capped pines
fringe the frozen lake
through the great windows.

I smell juniper, wintergreen
roasting cracklings.
pick up the fragile moth,
hold it in my palm,

finger the antennae, turn it over
        see the duller underside.

I squeeze my eyes,
squint to see shimmers of frosted light,
jewel-glass insect.
I feel heat rising in my belly—
surge of thrill beauty,
a soap bubble's
oil-in-rain colours.

I drink in this moment,
        hold my breath.
Just last month, Aunt Jane,
who lives at Bungle-Owen now,
sent a parcel in brown paper.

The artist, the one
who painted blobby pines at Door County,
etched angels into wooden boxes,
batik circus horses—
painted the gold-framed
"mother flying over the rowboat"
that hangs now under my stairs.

The card inside's bright picture—
girl with moth on her head—
the gift a hand-painted T-shirt,
moth silhouettes across the chest.

She's a "survivor" too,
had breast cancer twice,
sent me the girl-in–wings card.

What is a moth project?
A less-than-perfect insect,
second-class citizen
to the beautiful butterfly—
still drawn to the light,
resilient in its own way?

An emblem for the life-cycle—
egg, larva, cocoon,
transformed creature—
do moths melt to soup in cocoons too,
come out, after meltdown—
alchemy, radiant with wings?

In her letter Aunt Jane repeats
I'm a fighter.
I don't see myself that way, but
thank my right-side doing breast,
    nourish the quickening light.

What a shock this moth project—
bright, fearsome as a Luna moth
    caught in the porch light of dark.

Space and Light

*Sunlight looks a little different on this wall
than it does on that wall
and a lot different on this other one,
but it is still one light.*

*...We have borrowed these clothes,
these time-and-space personalities,
from a light, and when we praise,
we are pouring them back in.*
—Mevlala Jelaluddin Rumi, "One Song"

With musical accompaniment

for Anne Hurley in thanks for "Falling" song

At a window
she sits still and breathes—
'til it makes music

        notes
get lost
        inside her
breath is music

her musical
breathings soothe
like a seashore—

she rolls with the tides
        casts pebbles
into froth—

she notices
   stones
      pulled out to sea

ripples fingers
   like ocean

her music swells
and softens,
       inspires
then soothes

Fear, death, the whole shebang

is in that giveaway bag
you packed for the poor box

who wants those rejects anyway,
threadbare and stained,
missing crucial buttons

zippers that don't draw together anymore,
pockets with holes
don't mention blown-out knees

crumpled, folded and flattened
as if the ghosts have
left them, winded-out sails

they are merely envelopes
       with the invitations missing

just the husks of dreams,
the string left
when the beads slipped to the dance-floor

just think, you must
have been laughing as you danced
not to have noticed
the falling away of pearls

Most things will never happen…

the spark on a screen
means nothing
no trouble
negative

bumps
bruises
benign bits of duct or fat

seeds grow to good
go green, flower
do no harm

mostly—

a host of most-lies
I pray like beads
mostly clear
mostly contained, hopeful …

Most days I am grateful
this happening did
grow good things

that may now leave

Lilac

perfume on the sill
a mason jar, clear water
mauve clippings
from our garden
fill this sick room

purpura, periwinkle,
purple-cream and violets

colours that energize

sweet scents
lift every nostril
towards a brighting smile

as people enter
breathing ah lilac!

chemo smells of nausea,
red drips, chemical urine

clammy sea bands
on sleepless chemo nights

a lashed raft on kelpy swells

a distant foghorn
rolls in waves

ah! the lighthouse lilac,
beaker of spring in morning sun

Hairless

Bare feet, bald head,
this is me now

losing my hair in pinch-fuls,
my son and I laughing as we tug,
little fire pits of wisps on the tablecloth,
patches like a newborn's
cradle cap ...

even my vulva
        an open orchid

Is this loss?
                or liberation?

Let go of ego ... be bare,
where beauty is hidden

polish the brass lamp
for radiance—

daring
        reflection

in the warm sheen
my true self:

monk,
warrior

He Wishes for Snow

for John Mihevc

He wishes for snow—
to tamp down the rough stalks,
soften the spikes.

He wishes for snow—
cool flakes on a tongue that has sworn,
prayed, cussed, kissed—

recalling the seasons of snow-play
and sledding wild down the hills,
the Eastern star growing clearer
shining through tinsel and lists.

He wishes for snow tracks
ahead of him—direction for the journey.

Snow, not bleached with cranberry stains
from Yuletide tea towels,
but white as forgiveness
glittering under the luminous moon,
untouched, and
    just for a moment
as bright as one snowflake star-pattern
melting on the whorl of a fingertip.
    And so it goes—
ice to water to skin to blood
and back to water to sky to snow.

      He wants to lie in the stuff
for a muffled moment,   solitary
yet not alone. He wants to
snow-angel his arms like wings
      under falling flakes.

Light Up the Night*

You light the beeswax candle,
ask if I'm strong?

I look at the wavering candlelight,
little glints of mischief on a wick.

You are silent, a luminous crescent
of moon and snow through the curtains.

"Margaret is dead."

The Margaret I met at Bev's bedside?
The Margaret of the red balloons?
Laughing through Light Up the Night
at the odd white balloon of hope.

The one who called me
when cancer struck her breast;
whose eyes looked beautiful
when she smiled without her wig.

Margaret of wings and wine
walking Molly the old black dog
on the boardwalk
worshipping how the kids were handling it.

When Margaret slipped away for a while.
I thought nothing of it
when my email lingered in the ether—

my own tumour story, unanswered.

Had she moved, fulfilled
her dream of a wellness studio?

It never occurred to me,
even at my own chemo time,
when my son said it,
then took it back. To save me grief.

Annual Lymphoma Charity Fundraiser

Moon Tides

I. BLOOD

A single test: prick.
Bloodline, blood let, beads
black-ruby and thicker
than water, drawn
in family strands
that let down.

Three aunts, two chances,
two sisters, a niece,
one bosom friend
my only daughter.

BRCA 1 and 2 test—
one benign,
the other
a genetic black hole.

O Angelina.

II. MOON

Moon-tides pull
an ocean of seasons,
womblike pearl
nestled in dark sky
        starless,
outshine

moon and womb,
fallopian tubes
in a cave's deep folds:
        riven mysteries

an orb of light—
luna, luminous,
lupin, howling: no!

III. VENUS

orchids in utero
three babes in the caul
        I cannot speak for grief
if I ... (cannot say the word)

O those white sheets and angels
were ready for someone else

IV. HYSTERICAL

Desecrate the temple.
Cut out my ovaries if they offend life,
my uterus too.

I AM crazy hysteria, mad
to keep drawing breath.
O burning bush!

I do not need a bosom to love.
I have nursed my children
into everything imaginable.

I do not need a womb to love,
only a place
to lay my quarrel down.

Burn

Once at twelve
I spent a day
on the black slant
of my parents' roof
listening to Lighthouse, Chicago,
little bits of tar,
shingle embedded in my butt
as my face baked
to a later-that-evening
angry red, a later-that-week
brood of blisters.

I told you so was no salve
from my father
and my mom couldn't find
the aloe plant which must have
died in the window box.

Recalling that arc
of puffed and searing flesh
under my eyes
worse when wetted with tears,
I try to imagine what it means:

Radiation—
medical sunburn
eradication of cells
hot radar, laser light—
the doctor says

*it will feel like
you sunbathed for six weeks
with a hole in the parasol
exact to your breast.*

I envision the radiant sun,
think of its healing rays,
trace the incision on my right bosom.

Can I not skip this therapy?

Envision love and light
emanating from the source of all—
Healing Love—I blush,
nod my head, a *yes-girl* bobbing buoy,

the oncologist basking
in his own knowledge.

Space and Light

       click, click, click,
one mm post ...
splitting hairs
so fine

Exact science
on the table

You are naked truth
      your breast exposed—
tattoos and light beams
    lines
         numbers—

You, a constellation
measured, mapped out
      knit in your mother's womb
every hair on your head
      accounted for
You are stardust
with a dot of fear

Grit
    teeth
        be still
Don't move, they say

Like a NASA count-down...
        the radiation machine
orbits your body

What is a word
        for invisible light?

Only speak the word
        and you shall be...

Sophia

*Any consolation
can be enough to make you look up
at the yellowed leaves of the apple tree, a few
that survived the rains and frost, shot
with late afternoon sun.*

*…and everything
you dread, all you can't bear, dissolves
and, like a needle slipped into your vein—
that sudden rush of the world.*
—Ellen Bass, "Any Common Desolation"

Triptych for my Children during Chemo

WINGS

The tops stair moans
in moonlit dark,
oaken weight leans
on the lintel—I lurch—
stumble descending the stairs.

And Gabriel my angel is there,
his sturdy hold under my arms
rights me
after my fall, I lean on him.

EGGS

Yellow bile and bright sun
makes stark my bedspread.
I wake to spy
a glass bowl of water
filled with floating flowers.
Glints of morning sun
speck the walls.

Locky knocks softly,
bringing me eggs, sunny-side-up,
with twin toast and tea,
tells me he likes it
when I'm vulnerable
so he can help.

SWEEP

Lemon smells cleaner
than chlorine bleach with zest;
oh happy kitchen
when Annie wipes away the grime.

She is careful and meticulous,
her prayer becomes a cloth.
She says we need a clean sweep—
to make space, confess and let go.

There is a time for Veronica's napkin,
and a season for rags
to flap joyous purpose in the sun.

Frequently Asked Questions #3

for my Wellspring Community

Will my cancer come back?

We are in a circle of "survivors."
I dislike that word,
the war-ishness of it, battle,
weapons, contest in it. No,
we are in a circle of care.

Circular symbol
of all things shared—
no top or bottom,
start or end—
an infinite shape,
smooth and curved
as sapling vine
or greening garland.

Eyes closed,
we breathe
in light, each
exhalation expels a question.

The circle settles,
jaws slacken, space
for inward smiles.

We are at Wellspring—

a place to safely drop
our buckets deep
into places of seeping water,
        draw them to the light.
Still, sometimes queries
bubble up: *Will cancer return?*

Does sunshine?
        does drought?

We come back to the breath,
each one dissolves
symbols shimmering
below surface.

        The circle expands
and contracts—
        a living thing—
we make space
for those who come and leave

returning to the breath,
the give-and-take of it.

We fill and empty,
fill again

as each breath
expands us into
the great paradox—

fully here now
we accept the present
let go as well—

we return to the breath.

Vox

The sound of a voice,
  a rasping cry, is my own.

I am awoken, snapped
from a dream of desert-parch,
salt grains of sleep
still in my eyes.

Face hot, each night
sweats—the "ah" sound,
like an old talkie film
clipped, slapping in circles.

Cracked clay-voice;
moisture sucked
by radiation's sun.

I am burnt,
my voice box
a planter for cactus,
every sound a lump
of crumbled earth,

I cannot speak a river.
Dried saliva shushes me.

Pelican

I am pelican-mother,
pouch-pocket beneath my beak
full of silverfish, rush stems.

My feathered breast white
as crisp origami paper.

In times when fish are scarce,
I pluck featherlets
from my great chest
'til red comes in splatters.

Lines and circles
streak my bib—

my own flesh
gives up a feather quill-pen.

I blot the spots
where words come crimson
from my four-chambered inkwell.

I feed my young,
lift off
when the words are dry.

Ritual Blessing for my Womb

for Becca, Susie and Sue

Round, full, waiting, a non-pregnant Madonna, a vessel, goddess.
Fire in my belly and green of heart. A certain undertow coming,
I'm on an ocean wave climbing back in frothy fingers.
I will leave my nets on the shore, open my heart, give thanks…
Two dear friends bless my womb with melted snow, beeswax candles,
a smooth stone, tiny feather, give it leave-taking, safe passage and
thanks for the ark and covenant within it—trinity of children.
A gush of light, salt-sea tears, fierce juices. Joy.
As Hildegard of Bingen said, *may I stay green and moist.*

The magic is in the salt, they say

A pinch of salt in course-ground coffee,
a dash of salt in hot chili cocoa.

Like king Thrushbeard's tale,
one daughter's simple truth,
I love you like fresh meat loves salt.
His tears.

White sand on the table,
bright snow on dirt,
diamonds among coal—
salt is the secret.

A pinch accents flavour.
A good cry clears the head.

I'm sipping spice chocolate
after a text from my son
that his girl has dumped him.

He's been crying.
The chili pepper bite stings my nose.
I get watery. One drip
of saline plops into the brew.

Communion water mingling with wine.
Wanting it over for him—
the great wells of grief
that have begun to swell.

How can I hold his sorrow?
This shared secret,
the honor and weight.

His first love, sex, heartbreak.
I know salt in the wound
will make his life richer,
how can I tell him this?

Photo: Old Woman Staring at Hands

by Louise Burgereau

I am right back where I started,
watching my hands as if not my own,
ten inchworms dangled into focus,
or two oak leaves hung in my autumn face.

I knew them before I could use them,
their point-able, clap-able, suck-able digits
delighted. I know them well,
the skin they have soothed,
soil they crumbled,
shards, suds, slop and prayers
they have petitioned.

They tremble, tremble,
wave, droop, disconnected from me.

Of all the prophet portraits, palm up,
"Be not afraid, I come in peace,"
is this what dis-ease is telling me?

Parkinson's, you prevent
me from needlepoint, baking,
picking up pebbles—
make me let go.
I lean back and let
the quaking be a kind
of fearsome reverence.

Writer all my life: heart,
thought, blood, ink, pen
flowing onto paper,
I spoke words when my
right hand failed,
scribes scribbled words for me.

One day letters sifted into shaking
patterns, collages kaleidoscoped.

I could not hold them still,
moved my hands to shadow-play—
cross thumbs, spread fingers—the eagle.

winter moon at night

Winter moon at night
Yellow slit in fabric
Owl's eye blinking down

I am sure
the shore forgives
the moon nightly
for ripping her out
to sea and back

Sophia

I sit at her knees,
wise woman weaver,
ask this question:
how can I forgive?

Our elder leans into the fire,
stirs coals with a stick,
gazes into the licking dance of flames
with faraway eyes.

> *You ask the seventh question.*
> *I address you only, she begins.*
> *There are many means to medicine,*
> *spokes to the wheel.* She pinches herbs
> *from a pouch and flicks them into the fire:*
> *a burst of sparks and sweet smells.*

> *You have walked the labyrinth,*
> *changed paths, eaten greens,*
> *deciphered dreams,*
> *made peace with your father,*
> *held hands with your mother,*
> *sweetened the circle of siblings drawn closer—*

> *written words,*
> *hummed sacred songs, unpacked*
> *many things from your satchel,*

*eased yourself and others from petty things,
pointed words—*

    *gone back to the crack
you squeezed through to say thanks,
and harder yet, have received
when there was no way to give back.*

    *You have wept alone for nights,
wakened surrounded in mornings ...*

Now she sits silent, still,
bile rises to my throat,
I know this lump,

    I address you only, she leans into me,
eyes ablaze, but soft,
*it is not your love-bumbling mate,
nor his mother in her guilty kitchen,*

*not even the great male paws
that have pressed, pushed down, prohibited
the feminine through the ages--*

*you have raged all your life
against unseen beasts,
lay your quiver and quarrel down.*

Look into the still pond.
See your reflection,
past pebbles, sunken to the bottom.

You are enough,
just as you are.

Ode to my Vagina

O sea tulip, you
Were once squid-soft
And warm as shallow ocean at noon
A Gentle surf folding inward
And inward within you.
Your lapping petals opened
To welcome one soft sea creature
In your oyster centre

You were once swelling flower anemone,
Invisible cilia sweeping in
'Til seawater gushed, pulsed
Undulating kelp

But now you are beached
Dried as sea-racks of dilate strips in the sun
You are a sand stranded conch
Far from life giving liquid
Your whorls hardening
To driftwood—
Dry and rough now
As a bristly mat
The welcome word wiped right off

Sprout
post chemo

Like that grade one bean project
in a decorated Dixie cup,
those little unfurlings of green
poking up in the window,
      something is growing
on the smooth garden of my scalp.

Exotic as first fiddleheads,
little lines of white-tipped dark spike up.

Not pirate stubble
or coarse hairs shaved mean,
these are baby-fine, kitten fur.

I cannot stop stroking these soft tassels
as I smooth a palm over my crown,
it's soothing to feel something grow.

I do not speak the language of warrior,
had not helmet or sword;
I was shorn more as monk, stripped naked,

I have no head for battle, but carry
a banner for all people,

I want to stand
on this mountain's bald top
in the fierce, refreshing wind,
      waving my flag in the light.

Radiant

"Make of yourself a light,"
said the Buddha,
before he died.
I think of this every morning
as the east begins
to tear off its many clouds
of darkness, to send up the first
signal—a white fan
streaked with pink and violet,
even green…
—Mary Oliver, "The Buddha's Last Instruction"

Medal of Honour

I find it in a trinket box
between a butterfly clasp
and saint medallions.
It could be a treasure.

Its colours say Christmas,
red and green as poppies
on a legion lawn,
the metal disc like a silver dollar.

It could be a Yuletide military ribbon,
a soldier's lament,
or memento sent home
to a crumpled mother.

Reminds me of my Deda,
his stories of Amiens,
the bloody trenches.

The tale I loved the best—
after years of bratwurst
and apple pie à la mode
in a Madison tavern,

Hans, his best cribbage partner,
turned out to have been,
once long ago,
aiming directly at him
across enemy lines.

I think of my own cancer
that could have been war.

I think I will pray
for Hans, and my Deda,
courageous friends, no longer foe,
as I pin it on my chest.

Book of Hours

What time is it?
It is now, and sacred.

My son reads *Lord of the Flies*
on a small lit-up screen;
a percentage shows in the corner. 53%.
He is halfway.

His book has a half-life.
I ask him if Piggy's glasses have broken yet,
have they passed the conch?
I dare not ask
about the Valkyrie pilot's
flapping parachute
lest he's not that far.

I leave the instructions
for my surgery near his dresser,
don't tell him much unless he asks.

Last night he was my champion.
Stood up for me. Says he's glad
I'll be vulnerable--
So he can help.

I feel that's about right. 53%
At age 53, I believe I'm at my half-life

midlife, at the center
of my journey
midpoint.

But my life is not a line.
How can you be halfway through
light that never ceases?

No, my book of hours is only now.
In this and this
and this moment.

I am not Ralph, the lost boys
awaiting rescue, not wanting
to leave this tiny island
in the cosmos, blue planet.

I cup my hand to my ear like a conch.
Oceans of eternity in each breath.

A book is a flat map of lines and circles
that takes me somewhere else.

I am here and away.
A mystery and gift, this book of hours
       is not mine or ours
or in time at all.

Pages fan out, flutter
like wings on birds. angels, feathers falling,

leaves of stories that fly
on drafts wind and light.

White paper becomes liquid light
        then light itself
swirling around each story
        and coming back to itself,
dispersing prisms of brightness.

My son's face luminous
as he reads from his emanating reader
in a cocoon of quilts.
The moon full, her blue-white sheen warm.

From above

for Bev

You look so young,
your part still auburn at fifty
not a strand of grey.

I can see Nipissing freckles
across your nose,
standing behind the bed.

I hold your temples
softly in cupped hands,
your velvet smooth,
a baby's new hair,
downy, still.

It is quiet as a nursery—
hum of heat, tides of breath, a stillness—
fragile flowers' petals cling
like a portrait, hanging on.

Your perfect lashes, tiny
c-curve butterfly legs alighting
on your face. Each eyelash
fragile as breath; they too numbered.

God knows every hair,
knit you in your mother's womb,
calls you by name, Bev—
Beloved, your breath flutters.
We are bathed in tranquil.

I count the petals—
she loves me, she lingers not,
she loves—

each curl of lash faces upward,
as if to point to heaven.

Poem to my Son on the Occasion of Dropping Out

      Worse things have happened.
Be quiet, listen
for what your body is telling you.
Remember the time you caught tadpoles in a skein,
how it felt to hold slimy half-fish/half-frogs
sperming in your cupped hands? You always
returned them to the pond, patient
as darting schools of minnows
split around your ankles
to regroup deeper in the Bay,
by small islands
where jack pines leaned into northland winds,
roots tenacious in rose quartz,
their seed-cones split only by fire.

Remember skating on the pond
you'd shoveled off and flooded first, on minus thirty
wind-chill nights, you'd skate and shoot
'til your face was red and fingers white.

Back at the sugar bush,
you chopped a cord of wood a day,
carried tin sap buckets sloshing to the fire
'til the handles split your skin.

      You are no quitter.
You just let the season-songs
play through the flute of your body,
in time with the tension of breath

that now plays, now holds the note
for an instant. It all comes out music ...

In the end, no one will say
what did you get in Chemistry?
Did you finish Bio and Calc?
What happened to your first term?
Instead, they will watch you stand sure,
having shaken off the seizures,
wading deep in murky ponds
of brain, half awake/half asleep,
dreaming of a time your habitat would fit.

      You learned the greatest lesson—
pollywog potential of your gifts/limitations.

...and this is the end of it...

The dilapidated dock
that wharfs and lists to one side,
railing-less now, and sun-bleached,
timidly planking out to water.

Its boards, uneven as last steps,
or first, little catches of splinter and nail,
little shifts of lichen-to-wood colours,
one obvious depression on a slant.

This dock that has weathered
the snows, has known bare feet, shod soles,
has upheld dangling ankles, laughing like water.

What if I were to stand at this edge,
my toes curling like bird-claws
over the last board?

My Mom tells stories
of leaping off the peer
at Lake Clear; she is 84 today.

I stand at the dock's limit,
       look into the murky pond—
this is the edge of dock, of pond,
         one moment in time—

What if this is the edge of it,
and I never see 84?

The sun-warmed wood beneath my feet,
I stand straight—that sweeping
races from my soles to chest—

    I am here now.

Half Life

I hope in half-life
(the way uranium decomposes
at a slow rate) taking
a long, long time…

Carbon dating
Neanderthal bones—
milestones in centuries

I hope I'm in half-life this moment—
that my glass of aqua vita
is half full, or more

(life-force radiating out
like sun-spokes)

we have no insurance,
just now

four tiny x-marks now
where once my womb hearth'd

open as that field full of possibilities—

out beyond the *what-ifs* and *could-be's*—

a field of light, I'll meet you there,
half way

Son as Tree

This morning he asks
will I read his poem.
I am flattered, pick up the paper
penciled with words and scratches;
        a poem about mindfulness.

I think of all the clouds
in this sheet of foolscap—the rains
that watered the trees
that gave up this pulp.
        I see my Locky as a tree.

Fingers of roots reaching deep
into good soil,
he is sturdy in stance,
        grounded in his own skin.

Roots in earth, branches in sky—
        both/and.

He weathers storms well,
        many buds facing up.

Woodpeckers bore small holes,
wasps hang their angry nests, yet
his leaves draw a simple breath of wind
        that turns their undersides gold.

Proud white birch in the sun,
        he stands, accepts what is.

Water Music

for Rick McMillan

My kids are singing *hello from the other side*
for our cherished community music night.
Rick stands beside them, gently tapping the djembe drum.
Anne-Louise's hand on his shoulder, slipped into his shirt.

What is it about music that thins the scrim?

The membrane between life and death
already stretched taut across Rick's cheeks,
his eyes bright as two neon tetras.

Anne-Louise's lipstick a bit disheveled, like
he may have kissed her suddenly on the threshold.

*I stood with my three children at the Aquarium
under an arc of crystal just today.
Sharks slid overhead, separated by a mere line of glass,
jellyfish and mermaid's purses pulsing,
water pressed against our fingertips.*

Rick shimmers, all eyes, like the
father seahorse we saw,
tail curled 'round his young one
clinging to a shining stalk undulating in brine.

Moirai

On the Road to Mayacamas

It must have been fate—
right after a poem about you buzzards,
there you are, three bald hags,
hunched over and conspiring, high
on the wire above me.

You seem peckish today,
you flesh-eating dementors,
preening and poking black
tar-paper wings.
O Valkyries, stay

on the line, don't descend.
My heart burns, I forbid you
down-swooping and carrion-
lust, I deny you
access to my stance on this road.

Silent, red-tipped sisters
with hangover
eyes and wicked kyphosis,
I banish you thricely
your spin, measure, cut!

I, too, have known baldness—
known vomit and yellow flesh
baggy as sackcloth, picked at

bone-splinters, unfurled my bedspread
wingspan.

I know you are hungry, lust
after rot-flesh and things gone bad—
you smell what is nearly dead, and me
I am threading a string
of words now, measuring the distance

between you three and me—
Look, I will cut you slack too
and walk away, your not
noticing me
is your gift.

Just a Titch

is what I say when there's only
an inch of Malbec left in the bottle—
It's what I respond to offers
of dessert, coffee, sweets—
it's the amount of chili flakes
needed for heat, the pinch
of any spice to add taste—

Just a titch

when I'm challenged
on a detail, did I exaggerate
the facts? Was I frightened
by the turbulence? Did that guy
piss me off?

Well, just a titch

and when I dip into
the credit line, charge extra
on the card, skim a bit
from bills for treats

Just a titchy little titch

And when a space
showed up on the light screen,

a hollow bit in my rib, smaller
than the measure I always mention,

if you asked me then, the moment
I saw it, heard the impossible,
most probable reason,
metastases—

if you asked
was I frightened by the sliver
smaller than a seed, even
though I felt in my bones
all was well—

Well, yes, yes, just a titch.

Ode to the Radium Girls

You gals had the good jobs—
        painting clock faces'
half-past hands and numerals—factory work,
        steady and synchronized.
Orange Jersey bosses assured you
        the moonlit paint was harmless, so
in due time you decided to gloss
        your lips, tips, nails too with glowing "Undark."
What did the fine brush-points taste like
        when you licked the tips for perfect lines?
What seeped into your iridescent dreams?

Regular paycheques were fine at the time, but
        what of the studies they hid from you
as your jaws became hollow, your chins puffed up?
        Pride in your work meant you never missed a day—
never tardy 'til all you could swallow
        were short chokes of fear, hands trembling
as you held the stylus still, steadying your mind
        as poisons crept into your soft tissues last,
slow as Poe's second hand.

        The newspapers said the cause was syphilis,
cover-up lies sold in bold black and white.
        Did you even have time for sex, working
never-ending factory hours, you radium women
        who believed it safe in toxic times?

Did you gals even know you were called *the living dead*

    when you won your class action suit?
Did any of you live to see the brilliant effects
    of suing the *Luminous Material Corp?*
Your short lives stopped the clock for a moment
    on false fronts for profit.

The radiologist says *these days, rays are more precise*
    at damaging DNA, modern machines measure
to the millimeter, so only the tumour is irradiated.
    But I know about gloss-overs, money saved
more to settle lawsuits than seek cures;
    I'm wary about blasting cancer
with carcinogen rays.

I light a candle for you glowing girls,
    it smells of perfumed paraffin.
In my dreams I see your x-ray images,
    brave radium ladies, you who spoke up,
spoke up, spoke up! challenging even
    when you couldn't stand, or speak—
jaws dropped at your persistence.

    I too had no idea, when my blistering burns erupted
those bunker weeks of radiation;
    I spread marigold salve and honey
on red flesh between tattoos,
    both marks and melting permanent.

They say one can find your graves
    with Geiger counters, even today.
What will they say in twenty years
    about my own molten plastic breast?

I will write me a love poem

Self, true self, Divine Self—
Katie, beloved one.

A trinity of me, myself and I-ness
shining brightly
as my own happiest smile,
child-like and joyous

as my best-ever whistle
on a "just so" spring day,
greening with sun.

I love with arms flung wide
on a wing and prayer.

I sing myself a song
of my Self, three word
miracle:
I am Love.

I forgive the times I forget
this triple truth.

Katie:
mother, weaver, wanderer
plaiting three strands
me, we, us—all bright
with Divine Light.

Note to Self

Not a legend or map,
but a long list of gratitude
from grappling with switchbacks
on the c-country trail.

I read it now, at a peak,
feel I can fold my tent poles,
pack away hats.

Some where along the way
I left rocks on a pile,
spied shells and shoe-marks,
the backs of other travellers.

Cancer is a maze to self,
a solitary walk, and yet
the sun set shadows directing
my trek, and friends
left crumbs and markers.

Once with a friend we knit
a many-coloured scarf
to keep another warm,
once left a chocolate rose
for each nurse;

My mate and I have a list,
Camino Trail on top, camping,
carpet the squeaky stairs—
we continue it as long as long
as thirty years
or more.

You Can Lie Down Now

Dusk, the mauve-ink sky
smears down
        to dark ground, settles.

Light the twisted wick,
leave its wavering
        glow to evening breeze—

it will falter and flame its way to wax.

Melt your body down,
rest in this shrine of stillness,
        night birds looning into silence.

Smell the darkening jackpines.

As your body surrenders
to the earth of sleep,
        your cot becomes an altar.

Radiant

Dear Pris, I'll let you in on a secret: in the Distillery
before the Griffin ball, I was sitting on a fire escape
at the Mill Street Pub, and you jogged past in runners
and five braids, getting in a sweat
before the party dress and petit fours.
I stroked my bald head, admiring your energy,
beamed when you smiled and waved at me, felt
a poem coming on that stayed
tucked in a fold of brain, 'til just now.

Once I told you *I was holding you in the light,*
we were at Art Bar in front of the sound board, you winked.
I thought of a picture of you with a hundred tiny
Canada flags in your hair, of the champagne fountain
at the gala and the cookies with *poetry* written in icing—
thought of my own crimson-coloured chemo liquid,
and how it stung. You called your cancer
"kick-ass cancer" or something like that,
I tried to imagine my chemo cocktail as a beetroot potion
a hundred priestesses had prayed over.

And somehow your silver shining thread has been cut,
and I am still here, wishing something elusive.
I danced with you that night, looking up
at your face on the banner over my head.

Second Chance

Imagine you are me, watching the scrim
like Scrooge in a Christmas Carol—
audience for your own life, but able
to leap on stage, stop the action, jump
into the scenes unfolding
behind the curtained rim. Bravo! Encore,
but hush, what brief candle shines?

Imagine other actors, now gone,
klieg lights in your eyes, a bit blinding,
the radiance they left behind, the ovations
they will never get again.
They are the Shakespeares who left
folios for you. That you can make your own.

Imagine cancer words
saying *get your house in order,*
then, 18 months later, say *no sign of metastases*—
snap, just like that,
a set change, or lights out
and curtains up again!
Act two, your second chance—

So like that, ghosts, only living,
you could go back
to the bit parts in your past—
say thanks, and sorry, and clean up your mess,
wipe away the toxic spills, say yes again

to the musicians in the wings,
hug the front of house,
even the kids drawing posters
your lovely, lonely, luscious life,
greet again the guys in the aisles
ushering everything in.

Photo: John Flaherty

Kate Marshall Flaherty's poems about Ontario's Georgian Bay area won the 2018 King Foundation Award. She has been published in numerous Canadian and International Journals and Anthologies, has been shortlisted for Arc's Poem of the Year 2019, *Exile Editions*' 2018 Gwendolyn MacEwen Poetry Award, *Descant*'s Best Canadian Poem, the Pablo Neruda Poetry Prize, the Thomas Merton Poetry of the Sacred Prize, the Robert Frost Poetry Award, and others. She inaugurated Poetry in Union in 2019. She guides StillPoint Writing Workshops in schools, youth shelters, universities and hospitals; poetry is her lifeline. See her performance poetry to music at http://katemarshallflaherty.ca/kmf/. She lives in Toronto.

Acknowledgements

Shortlisted for the Exile Editions' Gwendolyn MacEwen Poetry Prize 2018 for "woman in winter," "Skipped," "Matrushka," "Dissolving," Chemo," "Fear, Death, the Whole Shebang," "Hairless," "Light Up the Night," Moon Tides," "Back to Moon," "Sprout," "Jut a Titch," Mushroom," Medal of Honour," and "You can lie down now."

"Ode to the Radium Girls" won the WDCR Poetry Award, 2018.

"Chemo" and "Hairless" were published in *Another Dysfunctional Cancer Poem Anthology*, 2018.

"Radiant" was possible in part due to an OAC Writer's Reserve Grant, for which I am grateful.

To hear Kate read poems "Just a Titch," "Tumour," and "Sprout" to the music of Gabe Flaherty, and "Sophia" to the music of Anne Hurley and Jim Videto, to hear the music for "He Wishes for Snow" by Anne Hurley, as well as to find out about readings, please visit her website, and the *Radiant* link, at http://katemarshallflaherty.ca/kmf/radiant.